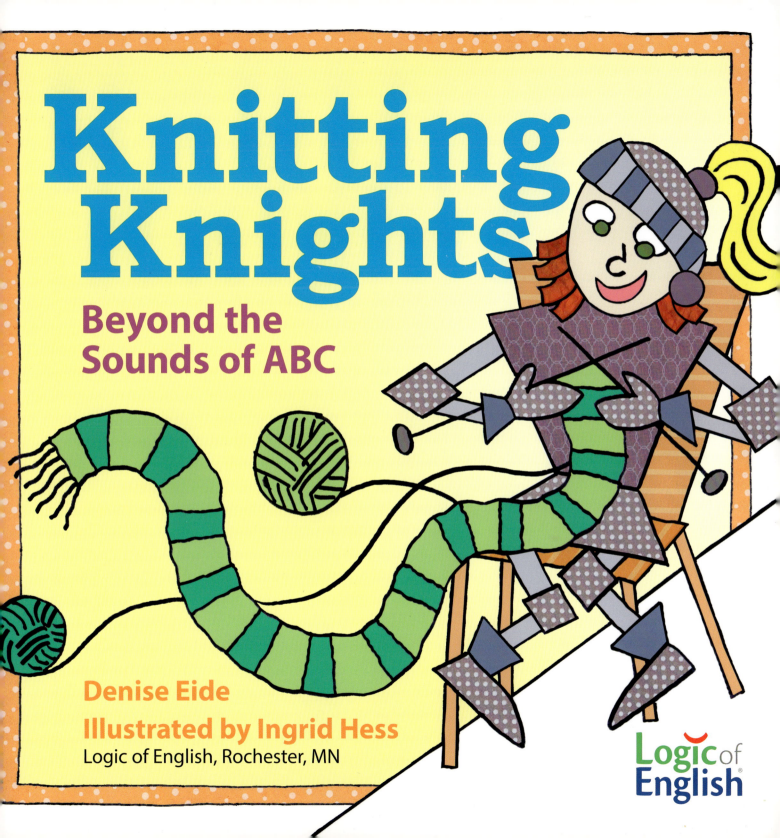

Knitting Knights: Beyond the Sounds of ABC

Copyright © 2017 Logic of English, Inc.

All rights reserved, including the right of reproduction in whole or in any part in any form.

Logic of English
4871 19th Street NW, Suite 110
Rochester, MN 55901

First Edition

Printed in the United States of America

ISBN 978-1-942154-14-3

10 9 8 7 6 5 4 3 2

www.LogicOfEnglish.com

Tips for Enjoying *Knitting Knights*

Help children develop an awareness that letters represent sounds.

- A phonogram is a picture of a sound. All words in English are written with a combination of phonograms. There are 74 basic phonograms.

- Point to the phonogram as you say the sound(s). Emphasize the sounds, not the letter names.

- This book introduces 27 multi-letter phonograms. These phonograms are taught in the Logic of English® curriculum *Foundations Level C*.

Sound Tips

- Many phonograms in English make additional sounds that are not commonly taught.

oo	/ö-ü-ō/	racc**oo**n	c**oo**ks	d**oo**r
gu	/g-gw/	life**gu**ard	**gu**acamole	
ei	/ā-ē-ī/	r**ei**ndeer	w**ei**rd	f**ei**sty
ey	/ā-ē/	th**ey**	k**ey**	
eigh	/ā-ī/	**eigh**t	h**eigh**t	
ew	/ö-ū/	shr**ew**	f**ew**	
oe	/ō-ö/	d**oe**	sh**oe**	
ed	/ĕd-d-t/	wind**ed**	tugg**ed**	pounc**ed**
augh	/ä-ăf/	t**augh**t	l**augh**	
si	/sh-zh/	pas**si**onate	explo**si**on	

To hear the sounds: www.LogicofEnglish.com/resources/phonogram-list

Encourage your child's awareness of sounds!

Birds twirl in skirts and shirts.

ur

/er/

Turkeys surf in hurricanes.

ear

/er/

Earthly **ear**ls ye**ar**n for p**ear**ls.

Raccoon cooks at the door.

kn

/n/

Knitting **kn**ights with **kn**obby **kn**ees.

gn

/n/

Gnats and **gn**omes on campai**gn**!

BUY NOW →

bu

/b/

Buy the **bu**ilding!
It's **bu**oyantly **bu**ilt!

Lifeguard in the guacamole!

dge
/j/

A smu**dge** of fu**dge** on the fri**dge**.

Hello!

Hi!

ph

/f/

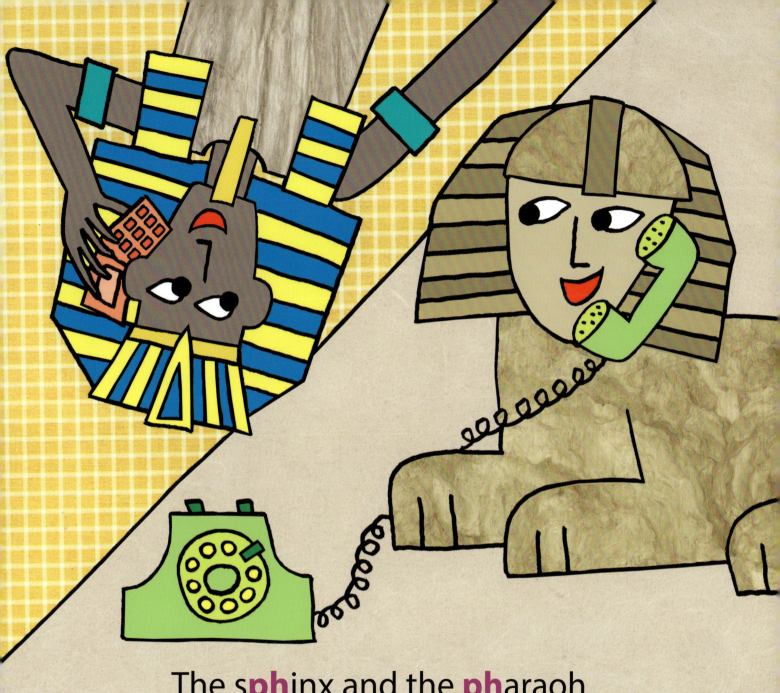

The **sph**inx and the **ph**araoh talk on the **ph**one.

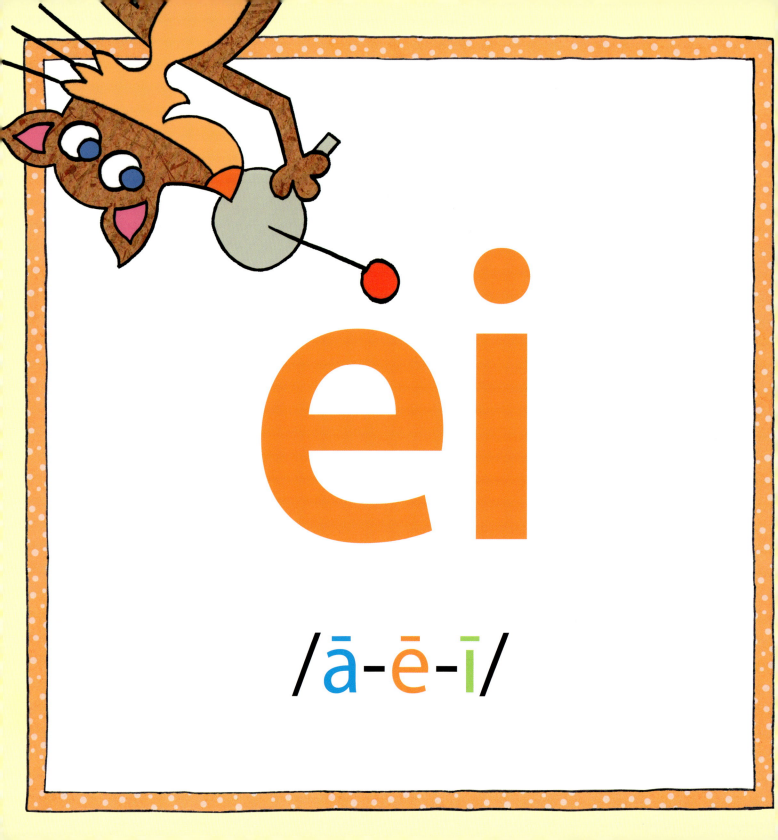

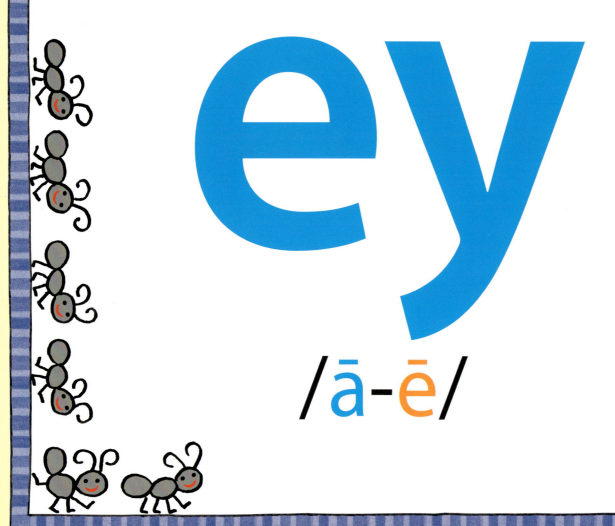

eigh

/ā-ī/

Eight giraffes compare their h**eigh**ts.

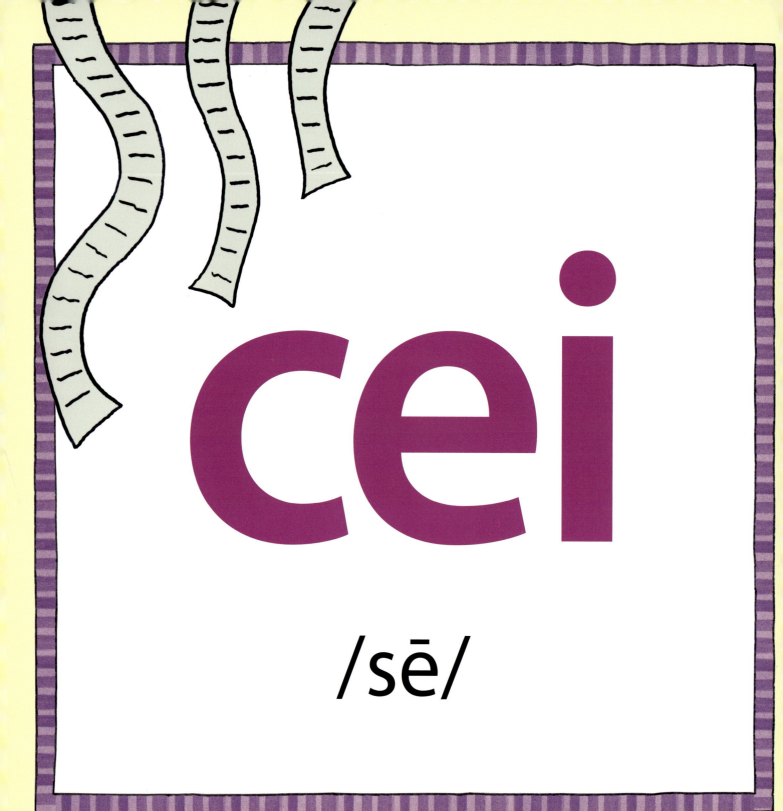

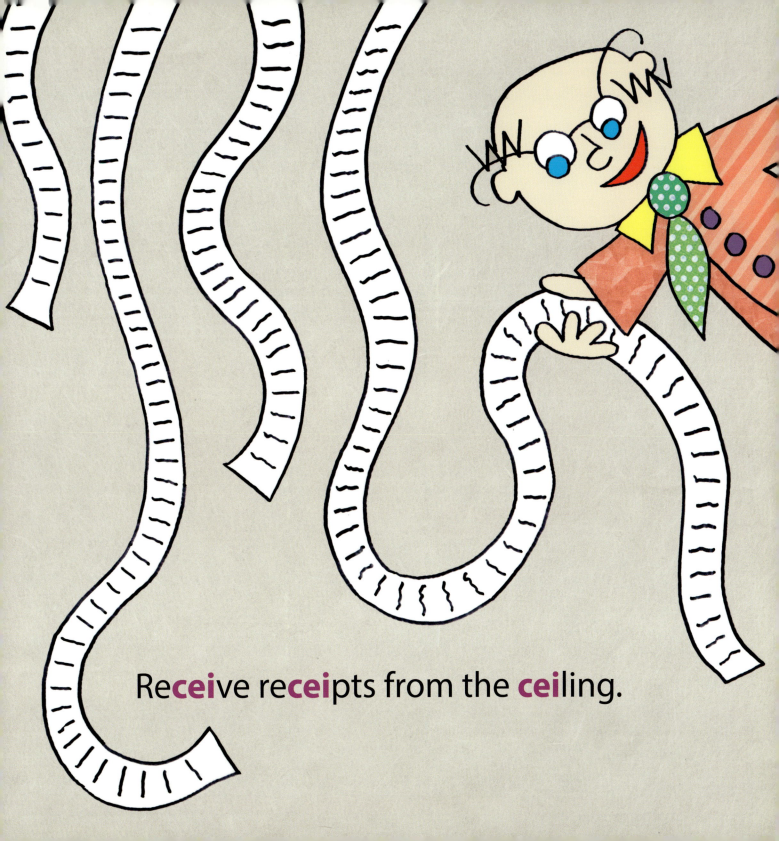

Receive receipts from the ceiling.

ew

/ö-ū/

The shrew interviewed a few of the crew.

Drinking fruit juice on a cruise.

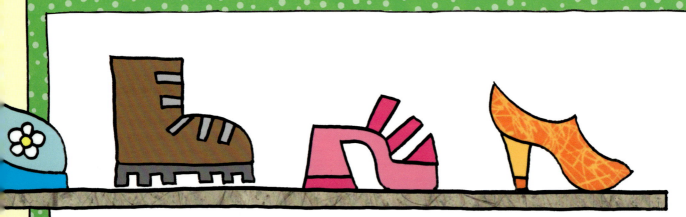

oe

/ō-ö/

The stylish doe puts on her shoes.

ed

/ĕd-d-t/

Winded pups tugged and pounced.

aw

/ä/

Awkward hawks sprawl on the lawn.

au

/ä/

augh

/ä-ăf/

Daddy t**augh**t.
His d**augh**ter l**augh**ed.

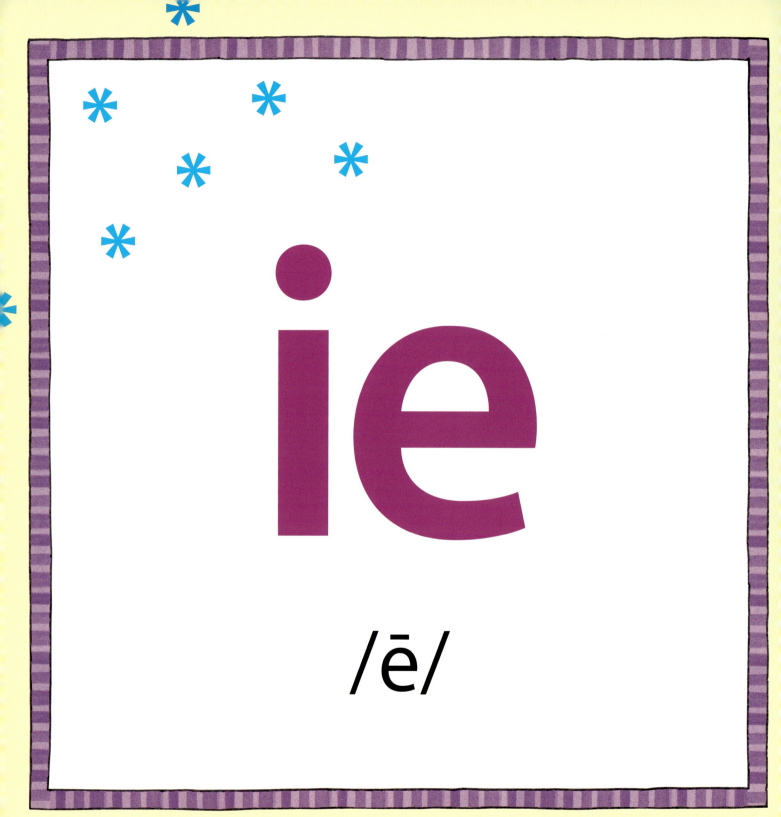

Pix**ie**s ski across the f**ie**ld.

Ancient musicians play on glaciers.

si

/sh-zh/

Pa**ssi**onate percu**ssi**onists hear explo**si**ons.

Emotional martians suction lotion.

Other Products by Logic of English

- **Doodling Dragons: An ABC Book of Sounds**

- **Whistling Whales: Beyond the Sounds of ABC**

- **Uncovering the Logic of English: A Common-Sense Approach to Reading, Spelling, and Literacy**

- **Logic of English Foundations Curriculum**
  A Reading, Spelling and Writing Program for Ages 4-7
  Levels A, B, C, and D

- **Foundations Readers**
  Levels B, C, and D

- **Logic of English Essentials Curriculum**
  Multi-Level Reading, Spelling, Grammar & Vocabulary

- **The Essentials Reader**

- **Phonogram and Spelling Game Book**

- **Phonogram Game Cards**

- **Phonogram Game Tiles**

- **Phonogram Flash Cards**

- **Spelling Rule Flash Cards**

- **Rhythm of Handwriting Series**

www.LogicOfEnglish.com